Don't Walk Out Now

Melissa Bratcher

Published by *Righteous Writers* Publishing

ISBN-13: 978-0692975565

ISBN-10: 069297556X

Book Cover Design by

Chantee Cheek (Your *Anointed Designs*)

Dedications

I would like to dedicate this to my Lord, Jesus Christ. To my husband and children who I dearly love and to all of those who supported me through this process.

Acknowledgements

I would like to thank God for using me in such great capacity. I would also like to acknowledge my wonderful Husband, Dr. Johnathan Bratcher for his love and support. Also to my beautiful children, I love and appreciate you! Shout out to my Aunt/Pastor Vivian Hart which is my mentor and who spoke life into my marriage. To my parents Tony and Lois Delk for without them I wouldn't be here. To all my family and friends from the West coast to the East coast. To my friend Prophetess Tomeka Bratcher of My Father's House for jump starting me to get this book going. To my dear friend Teacher Ramona Fairley for you supporting the vision of this book. A special shout out to Mt. Calvary COGFBJC, I appreciate you! Special thanks to Chantee Cheek (Your Anointed Designs) Also I would like to acknowledge Righteous Writer Publishing who worked very hard and worked right alongside me.

Contents

Introduction

This book is a testimony on how God worked through my marriage and tells the story of how we got where we are today. **This is not advising singles who are dating someone who is unequally yoked to stay in that relationship but to encourage those who already married.** If you are dating someone who is unequally yoked, I advise that you reconsider your relationship before going any further. This book also **does not endorse for you to stay in an abusive relationship**, if you are being abused I advise you to seek the proper help. Whether you're in an unfulfilling unequally yoked marriage, flourishing godly marriage, or a dating single, there is something for everyone to receive from this book.

Melissa Bratcher

Chapter 1

#The Honeymoon

"My beloved is mine and I am his; he browses among the lilies." Song of Solomon 2:16

Now, I know... you go on a trip, you celebrate and you consummate your marriage, this is called the "Honeymoon". At this stage of your relationship, you are in love and it's a blissful place to be in. Nothing and no one else around you really matters and you are both caught up in the moment of just enjoying each other.

The "Honeymoon" is the first stage of marriage. Most of the time, you are so in love you think that there is nothing they can do wrong and you want to be around them all of the time, hugging and kissing 24-7! In this season of your marriage, you may not have found out the certain things that they do that you don't like, (like ladies), you didn't know that he doesn't put his dishes away or maybe fella's you didn't know she doesn't know how to save or manage money; remember you are in love! Everything about them just makes you smile and you spend that time getting to know that person. This stage of marriage "The Honeymoon" It should be about just you two together (at least it should).

They can't do any wrong in your eyes, "they are my world, they are my everything" most of us say in the beginning! At this point, you really don't know what to expect in the marriage but what you do know to do is love and get in the swing of day to day life as a married couple. So enjoy this time of getting to know each other in the "Honeymoon" season of your marriage. I remember at the start of our honeymoon season, one thing we knew is that we loved one another. We spent a lot of days just cuddling and talking, and dreaming about our future, it was such a great start! I tell you that we had a ball laughing and just getting to know each other even more, I was in a blissful state of mind. During that first year, I just knew that we were becoming one and were starting our journey together.

"This one is bone from my bone, and flesh of my flesh! She will be called 'woman,' because she was taken from 'man." Genesis 2:23-24

This explains why a man leaves his father and mother and is joined to his wife, and the two are united into one. Two people collide all of who they are with someone else and become one with each other. When the two becomes one you must take what is left and make it become a loving marriage between the two of you. This is so important ladies because we are joined to him now, not our mothers, our girlfriend Tasha and them, no; our husbands or wives! This is who we should be connected to and keep certain situations personal. Same with you fellas, not Momma, the home boys or your baby cousin, just one another. Don't allow your Mother to run your house by telling her everything that happens in your home!

"Marriage must be respected by all, and the marriage bed kept undefiled" Hebrews 13:4

No one should be getting in your marriage to meddle about something you guys had an argument about. Go to your Pastor or appointed mentor(s) for wise counsel if you can't figure it out between the two of you. Girlfriends are cool but if they are not saved nor if they haven't experienced a marriage I would not advise for you to get them involved, but even still getting your saved married girlfriends too much information isn't good because they are not married to your spouse. When you are going to them "venting", it's not good to do that because you are sometimes painting a bad picture of your spouse and they are not the one in "love" so you could possibly be building a case against your spouse and now all of a sudden your family and or friends no longer like or respect your spouse because you have called yourself "venting". We have to remember that "venting" is a form of complaining and it is received as if you don't want to be with that person. To the outsiders, it seems you need a cheerleading team to motivate you on, "Girl if I were you, I wouldn't be putting up with that!" You know how that goes. Yes, ask for prayer from your sisters or your brothers but don't be so quick to always lay everything out and ask for their advice. Allow God to be the head of your marriage and He will lead you to the truth.

"When a man hath taken a new wife, he shall not go out to war, neither shall he be charged with any business: but he shall be free at home one year, and shall cheer up his wife which he hath taken." Deuteronomy 24:5

The bible even talks about the "Honeymoon Season". During that time, a newly married man must not be drafted into the army or be given any other official responsibilities. He must be free to spend one year at home, bringing happiness to the wife he has married. God knows best and it is so vital that you allow that time for the two of you. Ladies, he married you and you only and Fellas take care of your woman at all times. Esteem her highly because she is your rib. Don't allow people to come in and tear you apart, treat her like the "Queen" that she is. Now I am not suggesting you to not work for a year, but the point is to place each other in a sacred place, learning from each other and pleasing each other.

"Who can find a virtuous and capable wife? She is more precious than rubies." Proverbs 31:10

Ladies we must learn who we are so we can be that "Queen". I know when I first got married I thought I knew who I was but God will show you a different side of you that you didn't even know about, as time passed I realize that I didn't know myself at all. I thought I didn't care what others thought of me but actually, I did. I am teaching my daughter's self-worth early because it is very important to teach them how to be secure and how we shouldn't undervalue ourselves by settling. We are a virtuous woman because God said we are, hold your esteem high, we are overcomers! Men, be confident that you are a Man of God and walk in authority with humility. You are called by God to lead and with God guiding you, you can do just that! Ladies, you are Daughters of the King and Fellas you are Sons of the King.

In the book of Ephesians 5:25 the Bible tells us how a wife should be treated by her husbands for the entire marriage, not just the honeymoon season! It says, *"For husbands, this means to love your wives just as Christ loved the church."* He gave up his life for her to make her holy and clean. The bible also says she is to be washed with the word of God. Fellas learn how to treat your Proverbs 31 lady. Your spouse is always your first ministry and when you have to apply or preach the word of God it must be displayed to them first. Enjoy one another in this "Honeymoon stage" and learn here that everything is good but the time will change and this "Honeymoon stages" will be gone! When it is gone don't be too quick to throw in the towel!

~

Father in the name of Jesus I pray that newlywed couples enjoy their "Honeymoon" season. Let us remember why we married our spouses in the first place. Help us to stay in love even when the rocky roads come, even in the storms, allow us to see what you see let us love like you love with no conditions. Even when we feel like giving up we will seek you even more in Jesus name I pray, Amen!

Chapter 2

#The Honeymoon is Over

"Love bears all things, believes all things, hopes all things, endures all things."1 Corinthians 13:7

The honeymoon stage is coming to an end (if not already) around your first year or two into the marriage! This is the season after all the planning, the beautiful wedding ceremony, and the dress, all of a sudden this thing called "life" starts. Reality settles in and things don't look like they did in the honeymoon season. Things you thought were all that and right on point, starts to look a little different and seems like it is turning in a different direction. Now you're looking up the side each other heads like, "where did this come from?"

You are now starting to see some things that you hadn't seen before or maybe ignored in the dating process. It's like you didn't know these things about this person before but actually they are the same person from the day you first met them, nothing really changed but the status of your relationship. You just didn't recognize the flaws, or did you? Maybe you did, but you overlooked it and thought that you could change that about them. You just may have been caught up in "The Honeymoon " stage thinking it was going to last forever and you kind of overlooked this part of the person. You maybe are amazed about this season because now you are having to readjust your whole life to fit theirs and this is not an easy task especially if you had different expectations. I remember seeking God out and the more I would the more my husband and I would be at odds, so it seemed sometimes like I was losing the battle. When "The Honeymoon" season is over, it's time to go to war. You have to tell the devil this means war! You can't lay down and play patty cake with the devil, it is not the time or the place. It's time to put your war clothes on and fight the good fight!

Even when times get rough, I had to submit to God and second submit to my husband. I didn't know that when spiritual warfare would kick up, all of that cute and cuddly stuff would go out the window between us two. When it was time to fight spiritually, for a while I had to do it by myself, I had to go to church even when he didn't. Don't sit and wait for them to go to church because now you are both in error, go if that means going by yourself! My children and I would go on without him. When I got home from church, I tried to not pressure him by overly mentioning church unless he would ask. The challenging part of my husband being a backslider was that I still had to submit to him. You might be thinking, "oh really?" Yes really, you have to submit. "But he is not following Christ, but I still have to submit?" Yes indeed! Am I encouraging you to do a crime or anything unlawful? No, what I am saying is follow and submit to his command, because he is your authority and you have made a covenant with this person. Still, treat your husband as your king even when he is acting like a joker, he will take notice of how you treat him. Sometimes women talk to their husbands with disrespect when they don't have it all together. We can tend to want to talk crazy to him when your best bet sometimes is just to let it go! It is important to know that a woman is not to rule over her husband. The woman is the weaker vessel and the woman came second, from the man's side. Because of the fall, the man is the head of the household and leads the family. This sounds negative in today's society, but actually, it sets the women up to be blessed.

If we can understand the order of God and His plan He has for us, we would understand that we are so blessed by God! The Jesus said if you do it to the least of these, you do it unto me.

"*The King will reply, 'Truly I tell you, whatever you did for one of the least of these brothers and sisters of mine, you did for me.*" Matthew 23:40

"*So the last will be first, and the first will be last.*" Matthew 20:16

God favors women because we will ponder and pray over our families, we sacrifice for our families, we bear children and endure great pain. We are more than conquerors through Christ Jesus, we are not the problem, but we are the solution. Just like Mary, the bible says she ponder these things in her heart, we should hold on to the word that the Lord has given us. Our heart's desire should be that our family be saved and to be whole. Ponder on the great things and ask the Lord to help you through the rough times.

Fellas you are the head of your household. Walk in the authority that God has given you, not in an overbearing way but a God fearing way. The order is God first the husband, the Wife then the children. If you know the Lord you must stay in your lane and follow accordingly.

Whoever is out of line or out of order the Lord will skip over you and bless the one that is in the right place. In this union, try to evangelize to this person. Well, how can I do that? You got to love that person as they are, you have to pray for them constantly interceding on their behalf asking the Lord to forgive them for they know not what they do, just like Jesus does for us whenever we fall short. We have to love the hell out of them, literally! Also, remember your family is always your first ministry, I learned that early on in my marriage. There was a time that I wanted to join the choir at my church and I didn't have transportation to get there and I was really upset about it thinking that if I love the Lord why can't I go serve in the church? I called my Aunt which is one of my mentors and I explained to her what was going on and she gently rebuked me and said, "You have to tend to your family first and then if it permits for you to get a ride and everything lines up then you can serve at the church." So basically your family is your first priority then you can serve the church. Your family should represent you and you represent Christ. Since I was not able to get a ride to the church because my husband was out with the car or we didn't have a vehicle at times, I had to think of the wellbeing my family first. So many of us are not taught that, even if you are called to do ministry, your first ministry is your family. We often put the ministry first because we think it is pleasing God, but God gave you a family to minister to first. The word will always be tested so let it be worked out within your household before you go running out to start a ministry, let God lead you.

I spent a lot of time in prayer, hours in my secret place praying for my husband. He was gone a lot so I had nothing but time to pray. Praying for his safety, praying for him to come back to Christ. I knew that he was the man that I prayed for even though it didn't look like it. He is the Godly husband I just chose to believe God for and I would begin to prophesy to the situation. I would constantly tell him I prayed for a Godly husband and he would always say, "Well I am not the one!" I would rebuke the enemy and still declare what the Father said about him. You have to tell the enemy what the Lord said, declare and decree that thing and believe in your heart for it to be true. In a particular heated discussion we had, I started to speak in tongues and pray over my house and my husband thought I had lost mind! He said, "This woman is crazy!" The spirit of the Lord would lead me to anoint my whole house with oil and I would tell that devil to get out of my house. You can't let the enemy feel welcome in your house you have to let him know that he is not welcome and that he has to go. Send him his eviction papers, serve him and don't stop there, kick him out!

The enemy hates marriages. The Bible tells us about the power of agreement and that the power of agreement moves mountains. The word says, one can put a thousand to flight 2 can put ten thousand to flight. It's talking about demons moving them out of your way. They are trying to stop the will of the Lord but we must be in agreement to establish this. If I am saved and walking with the Lord and he isn't how can we come together in agreement? John 1:5 it says, "And the light shines in darkness, and the darkness comprehended it not". In other words, stop trying to "preach to the choir." You are pushing them further and further away because you are talking foolishly to them.

"They cannot comprehend anything you are saying because they are in darkness and you are walking in the light". Titus 3: 1-3

Proverbs 9:7-8 talks about correcting a nonbeliever is an insult. It will cause them to hate you. The only thing you are responsible for is to walk out your own salvation with fear and trembling. In other words, display it in your own life. Allow the Spirit of God to move through you and watch the Holy Spirit began to cause a conviction through your love and willingness to do what is right. Ministering to your spouse doesn't always mean preaching with words but by being a living epistle walking it out right in front of them. I encourage you to read the word with your children and take them to church.

Are you willing to allow the Lord to use you in this great magnitude? Will you be willing to go through long-suffering as Christ did? Are you willing to turn the other cheek when they have said some harmful things to you? These are some questions to ask yourself. Because if your answer is yes then you have to humble yourself and allow God to do the work in them and realize that it is not by might nor by power but by His spirit. You cannot and will not change anyone, so stop trying. Tell the Lord, "I surrender, I can't fix this Lord; only you can! I render them to you I will allow you to change their hearts."

Pray and get your scriptures together and war with the word of God. God's word is alive and when we speak life and not death we are ready for battle. We are not wrestling with people we are wrestling with spirits and it's the spirit of Satan. He can't do anything without God's permission so if God is allowing it, it is because he wants us to rely on Him to see us through. All things that come our way is design to help us grow, so continue to war with the word of God for your spouse! It's a rocky road trying to get to know someone and make two become one and it sure isn't an easy task trying to do that with someone that is unequally yoked with you, but with God, all things are possible to those who believe! I had to remind myself that I can do all things through Christ who strengthens me and he will bring me through this. I can't say this enough if you are being abused in any form or fashion I am not encouraging you to stay but if it is bearable and you love that person I am sharing with you how becoming in sync with the word of God can change you and your spouse.

Keep on seeking God in your marriage by praying, reading the word and attending church services. Never fight evil with evil, if they are being mean or acting nasty toward you, guard your heart because hurt people hurt people. Don't be moved by words that don't come from the Father. Cast down any high thing that exalts itself above the knowledge of Christ and pull it down and tear it down. When you don't receive it, it can't take root! You have the power through Jesus to abort that assignment so you won't conceive it. I encourage you to be reminded of the grace of God over your life in relation to your marriage. The grace of God is giving us what we don't deserve and mercy is not giving me what we do deserve. I deserved to be punished because of my sinful nature, I deserve to go to hell because of my sins but because He loved me and I received Him I am pardoned. I am saved because of His Grace when he hung on that cross! Where would I be without Him? So when we realize that we did wrong and we were forgiven we must know we must do the same for our spouses. Love covers a multitude of sin, so let's love them to life!

~

Let's pray, Father in the name of Jesus I pray that my brothers and sisters can make it through the rough seasons. Seasons of hard times seasons of not knowing what to do give them the wisdom so they will know how to overcome. In Jesus name Amen!

Chapter 3

#So Gone

"Let us not become weary in doing good, for at the proper time we will reap a harvest if we do not give up." Galatians 6:9

Even though we got married in 2003, it all started over 20 years ago when we met in 1996. A mutual friend had introduced my husband to my brother. The friend was in the Military and my brother was also in the military. The friend stressed on how important it was for my brother and Johnathan (my now husband) to meet, it was an urgency because he was getting ready to be deployed so he made an effort to make it happen before he left the state of North Carolina. Once they met, they hit it off immediately and shortly after meeting, my Brother's wife at the time had an uncle who passed away and he needed someone to help him drive to the west. So Johnathan willingly helped him drive to the funeral. They begin travelling and stopped through Tennessee where I lived and that was where we met. I ended up leaving with them on a journey to the west coast. Johnathan and I clicked right away through our conversation. I knew it was something about him that was different from any other guy I had encountered and was drawn to him.

We talked the whole trip there and back, I would stay up and help watch the roads. During that time together, the Lord told him I was his wife (he didn't tell me until years later). He knew what God had told him, but he waited. At the young age of 18, we had our whole life ahead of us. Right after the trip, we became closer and I moved to North Carolina with him and my brother. We fell in love and had dreams of starting a family, getting a house and a dog. We had a connection that was so rare it was like we had known each other our whole lives.

Whenever people would see us, they would notice something different about us. We held hands and said I love you to each other all day long. We were so connected it is almost indescribable. We instantly cleaved to one another and as soon as we decided to get married, suddenly, things turned for the worst. We started arguing out of the blue and not getting along at all. Right after we found out I was pregnant we soon were separated before our first child was even born. Can you see the enemy at work? So while the separation went on, God was taking me through" a process". Stripping away so many things that were not like Him. I was being humbled and there was nothing I could do about it but submit unto the Lord because I asked Him to be the Lord over my life and to use me. So be mindful when you ask the Lord to use you because he most definitely will! I went through a season of significant loss. Before then, I had a great job and then that job ended; I couldn't find a new one because employers considered me "overqualified". I searched for a whole year and still couldn't find anything! I now had two children out of wedlock, no job, and was broken. During that season, God started opening doors miraculously! Right in time, I was able to get a place in the same complex that I lived in. Everyone was just as shocked as I was, I couldn't believe I was in another place that quickly without a job. Before depending on the Lord, I thought I had it going on! My heart was full of pride like none other and thought I had all the strings to pull to get me where I wanted, but now I was in a place of humility and had no choice but to obey the voice of God. Even though God provided me with a place, this was still a tough season. In this place of humility, the landlord showed me favor so many times and there is no way I could have made it through without God being on my side. The Landlord would work with me and ask me to bring whatever I had and to communicate with her so she could help. I had to do something I never did; let down my guard and receive help.

I was in a one bedroom apartment with two children and received nothing but favor because I could not have done it on my own. Sometime later, the manager was running a special for two bedrooms and it allowed me to have another room for the same price as the one. I was so thrilled to move even though I had to move the entire apartment by myself; I was grateful to have a room for myself and for my two children! Through the struggle, I was going deeper in my relationship with God even in not knowing what my next move would be. When I became discouraged, I would cry out to the Lord and he would hear my cry! I remember in one of my prayer sessions with the Lord, He told me that I wouldn't have to work again and that I would be taken care of. Right in the middle of my storm when things were at its worst, He spoke and said for me to stay home and take care of me and my children. Can you imagine me telling people this word I got from God! You have two children, no husband, no job and you said God said what???? I know it sounds super crazy but I believed God and I am here to tell you, I haven't worked in over 16 years and I have been taken care of.

During the season of humility, the LORD was preparing me to be a submissive wife before I even became a wife to my husband. When we reconnected and got married, I was surrendered to the Lord and even though my husband was born and raised in the church, he was back in the world. He had backslidden and wanted no parts of the church. His past church hurt, and rebellion caused him to run from the calling that was placed on his life. My past hurts and unhealthy relationships caused me to run to the calling, God called and I answered! In 2003, my husband and I got married but we were not seeking the Lord together which made us unequally yoked.

"Do not be yoked together with unbelievers." 2 Corinthians 6:14

For what do righteousness and wickedness have in common? Or what fellowship can light have with darkness? Paul tells us not to be unequally yoked with unbelievers meaning one saved and the other one unsaved, but it can also mean you both are on not on a path to seeking God together. When oxen are yoked they are together equally so they will be able to get the task done. Same with us as children of God, we have a calling on our lives and when we link up and tie up with someone it must be for God's glory not to glorify our flesh! Marriage should first be about ministry working together, when we are working together we are moving as one. The untrained oxen would be lagging behind if they are not equal and that is how it is when one is standing on the word and the other is standing in the world. There was always conflict because I had my light and it was exposing the dark in my spouse.

"The dark doesn't comprehend the light." John 1:15

We were in a constant war because I loved him and he loved me but there was always the disagreements because I stayed committed to following Jesus. He grew up in church and he had heard all the religious talk and he was not interested. Johnathan felt he couldn't live up to all the standards they had so he gave up on it. The enemy will often remember our past and will constantly try to remind us of who we were and what we have done in the past. People who knew me would also try to remind my husband of my past to run him away from me. So now, people are asking and questioning why he married me and stated that I wouldn't make a good wife because of the decisions and the actions of my past but, they didn't realize the mental damage I endured, the brokenness and hurt from sexual abuse and abandonment. Feeling insecure about myself and allowing the enemy to control me through that emotion. The echo of their voices was influencing him in a way that he was remembering our past of me doing him wrong. So here we are years later trying to make this work, yet we can barely get things going on the right foot. I was broken and then forgiven by Christ and now I wanted to just move on and he wanted to make me feel how I made him feel in the past. I had decided to do something different, I decided to believe God in the midst of being talked about. The moment that you decide that for God you will live and for God, you will die, the accuser of the brethren will always try to bring up your past to keep you bound because at that moment I couldn't vindicate myself. I could only cry out, pray and worship the Lord through it all. Yes, some of the things that I was accused of were true but I couldn't defend myself. God takes the vengeance in His own hands when we don't!

You have to learn how to tune out the enemy's voice and realize the truth about who we are in Christ. I would always say if we don't get the help we can't make it! I knew that we needed the Almighty God to help us through this rough season. It was a constant battle and there were times that he was "So Gone" and there were times I was so frustrated I didn't know if we would make it over that hump. I felt like I was "So Gone" but we were determined to still try, even though it was a struggle to keep it together. Sometimes the pressure of becoming one can get tough but standing on the word of God and standing on the truth, it will help you along the way. Proclaim the will of the Lord and say it with authority and be determine that

God will have His way. I started to seek out the Lord even further and asked that He continue to change me instead of looking at my husband's flaws and pointing out the speck in his eye when I knew I had a log in mine. I knew it would be a journey and hard work but I was in for the ride. I began to allow God to start changing me and that is where He turned things around. It was God's love that drew my husband to Himself. My husband had seen a change in me that he couldn't deny that the power of the Holy Spirit was living in me. God just used me to draw him and I am so humbled and thankful at the same time. I am here to tell you if you would submit to God and then submit to your spouse in love amid feeling "So Gone", He will show you that humility is power!!

Father in the name of Jesus sometimes burdens can get so heavy but in your word, you said that your yoke is easy and your burden is light so we receive that and we can trust you so we won't give up and that we will keep on going until the end, in Jesus name Amen!

Chapter 4

#Pray and Slay

"The fervent prayer of the righteous availeth much." **James 5:16**

Being married you must learn how to pray! Your best weapon in your life and in your marriage is prayer. I spent a lot of time praying in my secret place concerning my marriage and I still do to this day. When you pray, pray with an expectation that it shall happen no matter what it looks like. Come righteous and boldly before the throne of grace, not perfect but in right standing with God.

When the two become one flesh you have placed a target on your back because the enemy hates marriages so he is always going to throw everything at you to try and split you up. Instead of two becoming one his plan is to create situations to keep them separated by causing strife and division so they will never bond as one as God has established two becoming one flesh. You got to take authority over your marriage.

"One will send a thousand a flight two will send ten thousand" Deuteronomy 32:30

Now that is one example of why the enemy doesn't like marriages, because of "The Power of Agreement". The enemy would much rather your relationship end in a divorce, and even if he can't cause a divorce, he is okay with a separation within the marriage. When we are not communicating we cannot be in agreement. If you're aren't praying together the enemy has put a wall up in between you and your spouse.

Well, maybe you are married but your spouse is always gone, or maybe they are always in the basement (the man cave) and you don't communicate with one another anymore, or you are always hanging out with your girlfriends or with the fellas, social media is taking up your time when you should be spending time with your spouse. When do you have time to pray together or pray for your spouse? We have to stay in prayer because it's a constant warfare battle that goes on and somebody has to lose but it shouldn't be you or your spouse! Tell that devil where to go!!! "PRAY and SLAY!"! Every day is a new day wake up ready to fight the good fight of faith, for the Lord is on your side! Petition heaven with your voice desiring to see change for that person. Petition God through speaking it, journaling and expecting for God to move on your behalf. I had to wait on the results even when it looked like my husband was getting worst, I held on that I was to have a godly husband.

Don't let what you see determine your outcome because God is more than able to change a situation upside down. "Don't walk out now", not on the person you said I do too, give them the same love and forgiveness that you desire from God. Jesus is in Heaven on the right hand of the Father interceding on our behalf so we must do the same! I am not saying that it is easy, but I am a living witness of what prayer can do for a marriage.

I would continue to pray and serve the Lord and pray until one day, the light began to peak from the clouds. He started getting ready and coming to church with me and the kids. He was really starting to seek God for himself again, he started reading the Bible. We started to go to a friend's Bible study on Friday nights and this was a friend he met in the world and the Lord had called the friend out of darkness into God's marvelous light with the help of his praying wife! He started his journey yet shortly after had a setback and went right back to his old ways, but I didn't give up hope I just kept praying.

"Pray at all times in the Spirit with every prayer and request, and stay alert in this with all perseverance and intercession for all the saints." Ephesians 6:18-20

Prayer is your opportunity to talk to God, you would be surprised how many people I've talked to who didn't know God talked back to them. If you didn't know that God speaks to you, I am here to tell you that God does speak back when you pray. Maybe it's through other people, through circumstances, TV shows, books, a check in your spirit or He speaks through dreams and visions. However He speaks to us and we must listen to what He is saying. Go to God asking for a healthy marriage, ask Him to give you the right mindset, ask for directions, ask Him to teach you how to love like Him, ask Him to show you how He sees things. The Lord gave me a visual of the machine when you go to the eye doctor and they are checking your vision and they keep showing you letters until you can see clearly. That is how He wants us to see through our eyes in the spirit, keep on checking until you see things the way He sees things. We must check with God on his vision by going to Him boldly to the throne of Grace asking for help when we feel like it is too much to bear. He is there for us whenever we need Him. See your spouse through the eyes of Jesus, I am not claiming it to be easy but it will be beneficial. Learn how to "Pray and Slay" by declaring and decreeing as for me and my house we will serve the Lord! Declare and decree that no weapon formed against you shall prosper and you got to go to battle with your prayer life. You don't have time to go to sleep and allow the enemy to invade your territory. This is your marriage and it shall be established in Jesus name!

Pray when you wake up, pray when are brushing your teeth, pray while you are at work, pray while you are driving in your car, pray before you go to bed. Whenever and wherever it is needed! I cannot make it without talking to the Father and bombarding Heaven's doors with prayer. I need it and my husband needs it as well. Find some scriptures to pray to remind God of His word and to remind Him what he said He loves that. Just as a child will remind us of what we told them, they won't let you forget. When we ask the Father and remind Him of what He said it is a representation of a child asking a parent and constantly asking and trusting you and believing you when you said yes just not yet. We should be walking prayer warriors, Ephesians 6:10 says to "*Put on the full armor of God so that you can stand against the tactics of the Devil.*" You have the authority to slay the enemy, tell the Devil who is in control of your life and your marriage. You are more than a conqueror through Christ that gives you strength! "PRAY and SLAY" every day!! PRAY, PRAY, PRAY, SLAY, SLAY, SLAY and WIN, WIN, WIN!

Father God in the name of Jesus I ask that you teach us how to pray in your will. We desire to be intimate with you and we ask for guidance in our marriages. Holy Spirit help us to be more like the image of Christ in our marriage even when our spouses aren't on one accord. We will seek you out in all things. In Jesus name, Amen!

Chapter 5

Get Low

"Hu*mble yourself before the Lord, and he will lift you up.*"

James 4:10

"Humility "a modest or low view of one's own importance; humbleness. It is the act of placing someone above you and it is a MUST HAVE when it comes to marriage. It seems that you have your own idea of the important aspects of life and they have their own idea. My advice to you is humble yourself and allow God to direct your path on how you respond to the disagreement. Humility is not the easiest thing to do and I haven't responded humbly to everything, but trust me when I say a lot of strife will be dismissed when you do. We have to remember that Jesus who is God in flesh yet was the most humble human being that walked the earth. We must obtain this ability to humble ourselves and die daily to the flesh, remembering what Jesus did.

We know through Christ's humility and obedience even unto death, we are saved today.

"He was oppressed and afflicted, yet he did not open his mouth; he was led like a lamb to the slaughter, and as a sheep before its shearers is silent, so he did not open his mouth." Isaiah 53:7

This was the greatest display of humility humanity will ever see. Sometimes we must take the low road so we can live as Christ lived and to keep the peace even when you're the only peaceful one. Trust me, I know that that is easier said than done, but the Bible declares blessed are the peacemakers, are you the peacemaker?

My mother always told me that it takes two to argue, so if someone would be quiet then the other one cannot and will not argue with themselves. I have found this to work majority of the time throughout my marriage because when I say something directly in the heat of the moment, something just isn't going to be said right. Being quiet allows me the time to think about what is needed to be said rather than what I want to say. If you humble ourselves in a situation even if we are right, God will prove you right! In

"Humble yourselves, therefore, under God's mighty hand, that he may lift you up in due time. It tells us to humble ourselves under the mighty hand of God and He will exalt you in due season." 1 Peter 5:6

God gives us a chance to humble ourselves and he has given us the power to do so. Even though we might want to get the last word and we want to prove that we are right, it just pays us to take the lower road and submit to God. Maybe they are right, but for the sake of peace maybe sometimes we should take advice from Jesus and say nothing. If you can't have a mature conversation about it and if the conversation isn't going anywhere, step back from it. I know people in the world look at humble people and think that they are weak, but 2

Corinthians 12:9 says, *"My grace is sufficient for you, for my power is made perfect in weakness.*" God's strength is made perfect in our weakness so for the world it looks as if Christians are losing but we learn in the word of God that is exactly how we should operate. "Getting low" sets you up for high places. Sharing your life with another person and trying to become one, it takes a whole lot of "grace and mercy" and being that humble person. It has nothing to do with what gender you are, God wants both male and female to be humble. Sometimes we also have to be understanding, they might be a little stressed and takes it out on us. Allow them to calm down and have a discussion when things are in the clear. There will be times when you need or want the same treatment from your spouse so try to extend that practice.

"Because of the Lord's faithful love we do not perish, for His mercies never end. They are new every morning; great is your faithfulness!" Lamentations 3:22-23

Let's give our spouses the mercy that we receive every morning from the Lord. If you didn't humble yourself in the last disagree, its okay, get back up and try again! There will be times where your flesh wants to rise up and tell somebody off, but your spirit should say, "Forgive them because you are forgiven". It's something about when you understand that we have so much to be grateful for and how God is still working on us that is enough to give back what has been given to you without earning it but by opening your heart and receiving it. To "Get low" sometimes means you are the first to apologize for what you may have said or did in a disagreement. I know that's a hard pill to swallow but that is an example of humility. He doesn't want us to dwell on what is wrong, He wants us to focus on what is right and that He sent His only son to die in our place. As much as I love my family and friends or even my man but I don't think that I would be eager to die the death of Christ for something they did wrong. But Christ came down from Heaven sitting on the throne, lived here, died here and went even lower to save us. The bible said he went down to hell to "Sheol" and got the key. He went even lower, so what are our excuses.

Ladies, humbling myself to my husband, in the beginning, was the challenging part because he had backslidden and my bible tells me to submit to my husband! Oh really? Yes really, you have to submit. Submission is the action or fact of accepting or yielding to a superior force or to the will or authority of another person. But he is not following Christ, I still have to submit? Yes indeed! Am I encouraging you to do a crime or anything unlawful? NO, what I am saying is to honor and respect him as your covering because you have willingly made a covenant with this person.

Sometimes women talk to their men real crazy when they don't have it all together. We can tend to want to talk sideways to him but that is not honoring him as your husband! You may not agree with them, but don't disrespect them. Have a gentle and quiet spirit because that is what will draw him closer to the Lord (1 Peter 3:1). Ladies it is never be wasted or overlooked, in Ephesians 5:22 it says,

"Wives, submit to your own husbands as to the Lord, for the husband is the head of the wife as Christ is the head of the church." I am about to help somebody get set free and save their marriage, it just takes some work! "Get low" and get ready for your promotion because nothing's in vain! Anytime you have a chance to "Get Low" get excited because it sets you up for a breakthrough in your marriage and in your life. God loves when we can stay in his perfect peace when chaos is going on around us. Displaying humility right when it is needed, right when you should be getting your spouse told but instead you choose to humble yourself before the Lord. I am here to encourage you that it can be done just rely on the spirit of God, you got this!!!

Father God, I pray that the spirit of humility falls on my sisters and brothers! I pray that they will realize that the exaltation comes through humility, that #getting low and humbling themselves is a setup for them to go higher in you. I thank you right now in Jesus name Amen!

Chapter 6

#Love is Binding

***"Love and kindness have I drawn thee..."* Jeremiah 31:3**

The true LOVE of God will never lead you to a condemnation or regret. Now, lust on the other hand, can get you entangled in a lot of mess and heartache. Our flesh will lead us wrong and we must learn how to put it under subjection. The bible states,

"To walk in the spirit so you won't fulfill the lust of the flesh." Galatians 5:16

Our flesh is in contrast with our spirit man and it is important to keep your mind on Christ even in your marriages. In relation to your marriage, are you willing to allow the Lord to use you in this great magnitude? Will you be willing to go through long-suffering as Christ did? Are you willing to turn the other cheek because they have said some harmful things to you? These are some questions to ask because if your answer is yes then you have to humble yourself and allow God to do the work in them and realize that not by might nor by power but by His spirit! In your own strength, you cannot and will not change anyone, surrender it to the Lord and show your spouse the true love of God. Show them the wonders of being devoted to Christ by reflecting the love God has shown you! Make a commitment to God and to your spouse that you will honor your union even when it gets rough and you will not walk out now!

We know that being a Christian we have adversity but having it in your own home where that is supposed to be your safe haven your place of peace and sometimes that isn't happening because of the conflicts of you being saved and your spouse isn't. Wanting to praise God and feeling constricted or uncomfortable to do so at times because you might be convicting your spouse and possibly making them uncomfortable. The desire of wanting your spouse desperately to go to church with you and to live a holy life, but that is the last thing on their mind. Wanting to play your worship music or sing your praise song and you get interrupted with them saying, "Could you turn that off or could you be quiet". I had to remind myself that I had to still share God's love, even in the most stressful times in my marriage. I wanted to show my husband that the love of God is what changed me and I wanted to be so contaminated with God's love that my husband became affected by it. I can't say this enough if you are being abused, I am not encouraging you to stay but if your marriage is not harmful and you LOVE that person I am sharing with you the power of love in my marriage. With LOVE we can bear all things and believe all things. Trust God with your whole heart and allow God to do the work through you first.

Love is a very significant action word and some unequally yoked spouses aren't drawn to being a Christian or devoted to the Lord because we (the ones who follow Christ) don't provide that loving example like we do at church. The bible says,

"If I speak in the tongues of men or of angels, but do not have love, I am only a resounding gong or a clanging cymbal." 1 Corinthians 13:1

If the only time our spouse sees us being loving is when we are at the church and speaking in tongues, what kind of representation of Christ are we setting? If I don't have love, it's like making a loud annoying sound to my spouse and to the world! In the midst of loving your spouse, guard your heart. When the word says to guard your heart because out of it flows the issues of life, we should allow God to guard our hearts and to do so you must let the word of God filter what comes out of your heart and what is able to go into your hear. Don't be moved by words that don't come from the Father even if those words come from the mouth of your spouse, always check the spirit by the spirit.

"Casting down imaginations and any high thing that exalts itself above the knowledge of God and bring captivity every thought to the obedience of Christ." 2 Corinthians 10:5

Abort the seed of hate when your spouse is getting on your last nerve and plant the seed of love! LOVE, LOVE and more LOVE. Forgive, forgive and forgive again. Let love abound in everything you do. Come on my brother and my sister, let's LOVE our spouses to life!

"Therefore, be imitators of God, as dearly loved children. And walk in love, as the Messiah also loved us and gave Himself for us, a sacrificial and fragrant offering to God". Ephesians 5:1-2

In conclusion, I want to encourage you with through God all things are possible! I decided that I wasn't going to "Walk out Now" on the basis of knowing how much I loved him and knowing that this marriage belongs to God. I also learned to invest in the man of God I knew my husband was to be, which is who he is today. I've seen the inner king in him and loved THAT man until his natural self-caught up to it. When I said "I Do", I had put everything into this commitment and decided to stay.

Today, my husband and I are seeking God together and we are learning new things in this walk every day! My husband came back to Christ in 2010 for good and hasn't looked back. He was ordained in the spring of 2012 as a Prophet under the great leadership of Apostle Anthony Wilson Sr. and Prophetess Tia Wilson of Sure Foundation Community Fellowship Church located in Aurora, Colorado through Global Change Network out of Colorado Christian Fellowship Church in Aurora, Colorado. Then he was ordained as an Elder at The Potter's House of Denver under the leadership of Dr. Chris Hill Sr. and Lady Joy Hill in Denver, Colorado. Currently, he is the Pastor of Mt. Calvary C.O.G.F.B.J.C Inc. in Raeford, NC. He also has a doctoral degree of divinity where he graduated from The Bible Institute of America located in Raeford N.C under the Ownership of Apostle William and Pastor Vanessa McPhaul. God is so good and He is faithful and guess what? He is not done with us yet!

Father in the name of Jesus, I pray that your people will learn how to LOVE like you LOVE to see their spouses the way you see them. Give them the peace in their relationship and give them the wisdom to know how! To give them the wisdom to stand on your word. In the name of Jesus we pray, Amen.

Don’t Walk Out Now

If you are involved in domestic violence or abuse please seek help. Please call the toll free hotline at 1-800-799-SAFE (7233).

∞

We want to hear from you…

If you…

Have a specific story or testimony on how this book impacted your marriage

Wish to have Evangelist Bratcher at your next event

Would like to purchase more books;

Please contact us at the following:

Evangelist Melissa Bratcher:

Facebook:Melissa Bratcher

Instagram: Serenityseven

Email: serenity7722@gmail.com

Notes

Notes

www.ingramcontent.com/pod-product-compliance
Lightning Source LLC
Chambersburg PA
CBHW072038060426
42449CB00010BA/2330
* 9 7 8 0 6 9 2 9 7 5 5 6 5 *